Fire Power

Other books by Chrystos

Not Vanishing

Dream On

In Her I Am

Fugitive Colors

Fire Power

Chrystos

Press Gang Publishers
Vancouver

First Edition 1995.

Some of the poems in this book have been previously published: "Going
Into the Prison" was first printed in *Out of Time*, the newsletter for Out of
Control: Lesbian Committee to Support Women Political Prisoners &
Prisoners of War; "I Lift the Pearl" was first printed on an invitation to
a benefit for Kitchen Table Press, sponsored by Herland, in Oklahoma;
"Corrugated" was first published in *So's Your Old Lady*, a magazine which
is now out of print; and "Late Breakfast" was first published in *My Story's
On*, an anthology edited by Paula Ross, which is now out of print.

The Publisher gratefully acknowledges financial assistance from the
Book Publishing Industry Development Program of the Department of
Canadian Heritage.

Canadian Cataloguing in Publication Data
Chrystos, 1946–
  Fire power

  Poems.
  ISBN 0-88974-047-X

  I. Title.
  PS3553.H85F57 1995   811'.54   C95-910662-6

Edited by Barbara Kuhne
Cover art is a detail from a watercolor painting,
    She Wanted Her Freedom, by Chrystos, ©1995
Author photograph by Ana R. Kissed
Design by Val Speidel
Typeset in ITC Berkeley Oldstyle
Printed and bound in Canada by Best Book Manufacturers
Printed on acid-free paper ∞

Press Gang Publishers
101-225 East 17th Avenue
Vancouver, B.C. V5V 1A6 Canada
ph: (604) 876-7787
fax: (604) 876-7892

This book is in honor of all my Two-Spirit friends,
from many of the First Nations, in Australia
as well as the Americas

In memory of Pat Parker, who sharpened my aim

For Joanne Garrett

For Prisoners, Comrades & Survivors
in the war against injustice & abuse

All of these love and lust poems are for Bọ
whose starship rides carry me through
whose warrior stance
inflames my own

Contents

Fire Power

Going Into the Prison

the guard growls, *What's this?!*
Poetry, I answer, *just Poetry*
He waves me through
with a yawn
that delights me
So I smuggle my words in
to the women
who bite them chewing starving
I'm honored to serve them
bring color   music   feelings
into that soul death
Smiling as I weep
for Poetry who has such a bad reputation
She's boring, unnecessary, incomprehensible
obscure, effete
The perfect weapon
for this sneaky old war-horse
to make a rich repast of revolution

for Linda Evans

You Are Not Here

Tender green buds of your eyes hidden
under lashes like winter trees caught
in sudden sunlight
Broad hands cradling my breasts
Your strength shining beside mine
These long miles between our mouths
shiver my lips hungering for your deep voice
muffled in my neck murmuring *Mornin' Baby*
I touch myself honoring you
as snow melts in random bouquets
Lifting my heart into the torn gray sky
over brown lace muted hills
coming in your warm arms as you wake
with a soft sigh of wings
drying in spring
& all we will make
opening in my hands

This dangerous disease, whose anagram stands for
I'm The Center Of The Universe, was formerly restricted
almost exclusively to the euro-immigrant classes but
has now made appalling forays into all levels of civilized
tribes. It is a difficult problem to diagnose, particularly
since the entire population is in deep denial about its
existence & there is great embarrassment in admitting
to being infected. Often, those with severe cases of the
disease will exhibit false modesty or sensitivity in an
effort to conceal their sick condition. While it is more
frequently seen in members of the male sex, it has
unfortunately also made inroads into the female sex,
including many Lesbians, whom one would expect
to know better.

There are a number of conditions which make the
underlying disease evident—among these are: inability
to listen to others for longer than 3 minutes; the false
concept that one's own ideas are superior to all others;
the pitiful belief that control of others is paramount to
one's own sanity; and a particularly debilitating form of
verbal diarrhea in which the patient cannot seem to
shut up. This researcher is consistently fighting evidence
of this disease in herself, not always successfully, since
the germs are everywhere. So far, the only cure seems to
be self-diagnosis & long periods of silence, growing
herbs. As we live in such an unbalanced way, it is
expected that this disease will continue unrestrained.
We may only be able to discover a vaccine if the current
medical and governmental establishments are completely
overthrown.

When one encounters someone who has a severe case which is undiagnosed, it is best to leave them as quickly as possible to their own devices, since no amount of arguing will convince them to seek treatment. If the sufferer does not seem to want to let one go, it is best to fake an immediate appointment with the toilet, referring to something one has eaten, while making a face. This generally will cause them to become disinterested in convincing one that they are indeed ITCOTU.

for Joanne Garrett and Cheryl Jones
who laughed so hard

Bitter as the Pockmarked Streets

which imitate my face as I walk through dog shit
jobs with a pleasant façade hiding my weary fury
Won't sell my mind to corporations or academia
so they declare me unfit to teach
I might say something to get them
in the trouble they deserve
Riding in the backest back of the bus so no one
can surprise me from behind
I open a cold window so I can stand
the stink of vomit & piss
of people just like me who haven't got
the knack of masks
I sit beside a young woman pretending to be poor
with torn jeans, green doc marten boots & a $45 haircut
I can tell at a glance that she isn't hungry
has never worked 10-hour days for weeks & weeks
so as not to get fired
Her hands & face are smooth with ignorance
Next to her on the seat is a copy of
Their Eyes Were Watching God
Idly I wonder if it's required reading
because this bus ends up in the university ghetto
where you can buy
arts & crafts from every part of the world
in a quest to be hipper than thou
which is like holier than thou
but you don't have to get up early
on Sunday for church
My earplugs don't quite drown
out the young men banging egos over existentialism

which I read about in high school & discarded
I've been cleaning houses for 40 years
Started with my mother's
Moved on to washing kitchen floors on Saturdays
in Pacific Heights for 50¢ each on my hands & knees
I'm still on them
but now my elbows are full of sharp razors
my joints are swollen   knees ache
I drink a pot of tea to get through a day
This beautiful mind given to me by Creation
has never been well used for more
than a few days at a time
What's the use of weeping
What's the use of breathing
There is no place to match my need
No relief from these beggar words
Books I could write
wash down the drain
as I rinse off comet
At least I've a roof to rent & food
Have to stop
writing this before I get up & start strangling
all the innocent young euro-immigrants around me
I count 23
Couldn't finish them all before
the cops would arrive
There's millions more where they came from
Twisted in rage rotting my soul I'll shut
up now like I'm supposed to

for Dawn Daylight

While There's Still

an edge to the parking lot

you can hear the orange gold

songs of autumn birds

bursting into dawn in an uneven

ragged line of untrimmed trees

You could

lean out

over the railing

which keeps you from it

& despite everything

breathe in the beauty

for Merle Woo

The Man Who Had a Lobotomy

sat in front of the nurses' station
at the entrance of napa state hospital
all day
without moving or speaking
At night they lifted him
like unfolding a bed
& took him away
In February the acacia came like paradise
I cut down branches with a stolen knife
brought them to him
He smiled
for the first & only time
The nurses yelled
You leave that poor man alone
Get back

Unsettling Poetry

His daddy taught him the difference
between trim & transvestite
Soul cold it's a long
time since I've heard that word
Back then I was
trim
Head full of scars bloody journey
away from being trim
Some places I'm still treated like trim
Street corners in Australia where they
like their tarts plump
Universities who are using me to prove
they're not racist or homophobic
Conferences where I can get run over
by the lack of Indians or Dykes
Trim is the part you don't need
Garnish not the real
biznez of poetry which is run
by the boys & their flunkies in skirts
Trim is the whore you can use & abuse
or kill if you feel like it
As Queer trim I heard the scorn
slightly covered in his voice as he said
transvestite
which ignorant folks have called me
Even in a multicultural poetry reading
you can get smashed up against a word like
trim
So in front of everyone
I claim it

When She

told me she
wanted another woman grief
went for a walk until
it stopped floundering shells
broke under heavy
boots rocks were holes
seaweed red fingers stones
were wounds driftwood collapsed
in bone fragments
there were tears or rain
graves were dug up
the tide came in with fast fury
storm in the water debris
that didn't belong
wind blew my head open
when she told me

Ground Zero

Raising myself away from nothing to eat for dinner
screaming sticks   silence snarling behind
locked doors that made sure
I knew I was useless, a pig, ugly, a whore, stupid
a no good damn brat who was going to be the death
of her & me if I didn't shut up
I make lists that say
Get Dressed   don't forget shoes
Eat Breakfast
Comb Hair
Brush Teeth
Breathe
which I sometimes can't follow
Cradling these children who pound with fear
cry for a safe hole
I joke that my mother is psycho
at parties where I'm sober as she still is not
She demands my tears for all
grandma's & daddy's cruelties to her
Her cruelty to me absolutely
did not happen   I must be imagining things again
Maybe I should go back to nuthouse number 169
Inside her failed attempts to strangle & drown me
I've lived
What I sent to the moon then
comes back to choke me now
I've some scars I could drag into a court of law
but I can't see her again
Just need
to see myself

Pink Snow

on stone steps

at sunrise

the cherry shakes

loose

for Y'ana Rosa
whose very first poetry reading
was one I did

In Oklahoma

your face appears in the bark of a tree
I've never seen before
with a dry sweet smell of your voice
leathery rough leaves serrated
Your photo smiles at a table
of half-eaten food wearing
your Butch jacket & a cocky look
clinging to my refrigerator since
you kissed a gun in a shopping mall
& all of us
good-bye
without a word
I carry you
to Winnipeg to Chicago to small
university towns I've never heard of
& you'd poke fun at
I am unraveling this message
you've left me left us
Suicide a word with no metaphor
a razor wire fence
that comes in my dreams dragging me over
We were children born into alien worlds
We share the scars of rape
our eyes old as slavery
On the back of this picture your writing
scrapes across   *Here I am*
in my favorite place, next to the food
& the back door
I've sat on your back porch believing
we'd eat together again

You are incomprehensible too big a word
knotted through my fingers
I stare at your death which calls to me
I'm not following you
My love bitter
slaps you so hard
You could
have called

for J Max

Rush Hour

waiting in the bus stop with a seat at least
when across the street a #7 Rainier jerked
to a belching screech so
my eyes rested on an extraordinarily
beautifull Black woman about our age
Her sloping cheekbones caught the light
in an amazing deep mulberry glow
I wanted to run through traffic
bang on the door as the bus groaned away
to tell her
You're the loveliest sight of my whole day
Thank you!
Staring down at my purple knees
I knew with such a hard ache
in my sore feet
that she'd just think
I was plum crazy

for Rosaura Diaz

One Learns the Ceiling

thoroughly
eyes jump from crack to crack
make meaning out of nothing
nothing helps
valium   codeine   meprobamate   traction
massage   sonic healing machines   shiatsu
osteopath   chiropractor   pressure points
reflexology   hot mustard packs
nothing
Pain moves in takes over squats always on the edge
hungry to knock you down
abort every attempt to think of anything else
So tired of the question *How's your back?*
I answer mindlessly from hurt *Fine thank you*
My face became a mask that shut everyone out
Used all my strength for a façade of my former life
How many times did I grit
my teeth & lift or bend thinking
it was all in my mind   Unwilling
to admit that I might be frail   need help
More than a year in & out of walls of agony
I learned how to work with a hot double-edged sword
for a leg   So that when he finally came
with the last resort of surgeon's knife
I heaved my terror to the corners
went under
endured morfiend every 2 hours scared
I'd return for good to the land of junk
weeks in a hospital of strangers
with allergic reactions

no Lesbian nurses   no Indian anyone
a lover angry because she thought she had to visit me
until I said *Don't bother*
rattle of TVs going constantly on different channels
food nourishing as wasp stings
being turned with a sheet like a pancake
my teeth glued to keep from screaming
Came home to a house neglected for a month
since I was the wife
moldy cheese in the corners of the refrigerator
& the news she wanted another woman
since I wasn't any fun these days
Everything put away in different places
by friends who had helped
Relearned the ceiling
humiliated had my shoes tied & untied
my underwear pulled as far as my knees
found out how to pick things up with my toes
began to walk   very slowly
bird songs thrilling each step
walk without pain
farther each day
feeling profoundly
the release of sky
no cracks

for my dog Beaumont
who lay beside me licking my tears of pain
Miss you old man

Breathlessly

she says that her friend saw me the other night
at the Club Confidential in a glorious silver evening
gown & I looked, quote, fabulous
I believe that at the time I was knee
deep in mud planting roses or perhaps
that was the dusk
when I shoveled sand over the newly laid
irrigation pipes as my brother glued & fiddled
farther along
At any rate I was over 700 miles away
I know better than to deny even knowing
what the Club is or having a silver dress
which does indeed sound fabulous
Gossip is made by those who don't write
their obsession no less fierce than mine
Of course I'm curious who looks enough like me
to be seen as me although experience says
she might just be another Indian (read any)
with long hair
or someone named Chris with brown eyes
Stories about me are far more fabulous than my true life
so I just let them spin out of control
Truth is so unpopular & muddy
but confidentially, just for the hell of it
I really was planting roses with dirt under my nails
a bandana to keep the sweat out of my eyes
& I truly was
glorious

The Roma Say

Bury me standing up
as I've been on my knees
all my life
I know this place
as sun rises a bouquet of gold lights
perfuming water of the Sound
I focus on the flowers
as voices babble
what they want
my maid's knees aching, my fingers curved
& swollen with scrubbing
I know this place
though I grew up hearing the word *gyp*
to mean cheat or steal
said it myself until you taught me better
Stealing is another familiar idea
I've stolen breath, time, women
Far more has been taken from me
as I've mimed a walk
from my knees
The water remembers us
We've never been savage in her arms
We know justice as a strange swamp creature
useful for murdering us
My mother said if I was not good
the Gypsies would come & steal me
I'd seen a beautiful empty Gypsy caravan
painted all over with roses
at the Sutro's Baths Museum
before it burned down

along with a vast intricate town
made all of matchsticks
by convicts
who know this place too
I waited on childhood corners
anxious to be stolen
from my life of hunger   beatings   shame
The Gypsies didn't come
This absurd disappointment rests
in a burnt town of memories
No water douses these flames of a child
who beaten down & with no home
hopes for a fire circle
surrounded by roses
where like sun
they'd let us be
off our knees
We know this place

for Morgan Ahern, Roma Woman

Sometimes Sitting in the Airport

when the normal white women
in pretty summer dresses
laughing eyes
bows in their hair
float by
burbling inane remarks
playful comments
like a vast bouquet of flowers
lilies of the field so happy
I hate them fiercely
just for that

Here's the Ruthless Edge

of Poetry who pushes delight demanding wide spaces
for herself with disregard for cocktail parties
conventions & the feelings of family and friends
who consumes our lives & hopes
leaving nothing sacred
She's a private pirate looting & burning
with not a polite bone to obscure
her desire to flaunt herself
fanning her metaphors
lively as the smell of dead fish
She'll tear your skin open with brambles called words
she's a fever that will break your dreams
she's full of lines you can't escape
She'll get you
in the end

for Minnie Bruce Pratt

Down Under the Taxi Yellow

street lights of Footscray
rushing through damp winter streets
to another reading my dirty socks wedged
between performance heels & masks
in the bag I can no longer close
I taste your hunger for me
as shadows flicker quick as blinking on my lips
It is the summer of your tongue
I want
with an ache as long
as these thousands of miles
between our bodies
Take me
through this strange night
into the sun of your hand in me
our hot meadow
where oblivion beats with a slow
opening of a swallowtail's wings

I've Done the Time

for the mother who tried to drown me
for daddy who cut open my leg with an ax
then screamed at my clumsiness
for their humiliations, hunger, hatred
beatings with anything handy
I've done the time for the man who raped
me from 12 to 21
while they've gone free
I've paid & paid women to listen
sometimes making a choice
between groceries & therapy
So deep in their hole
I thought anyone had a right
to beat me rape me scream at me lock me in cars
throw plants at me steal from me
& call it love
I've done the time until I don't
know when I'm due to go
hard time
while they've gone free
so I can't help spitting
when anyone talks of justice
You see me as smooth strong feeling my power
I'm still screaming
to get out

Hope Haiku

A young Black man

arguing passionately

with 3 white ones who are

not in favor of women's rights

Mr. Wind Dancer

was lecturing me earnestly in a heavy German accent
about the advantages of living close to the earth the
way Native Americans did. *Did?!* But I was silent.
I've learned to curb my sarcastic tongue which inquires
how one could do anything *else*—even if you spent
your entire life in a jet, you'd still have to touch down
to refuel. I was trapped in the sticky web of his
sincerity, watching the crows gossip in the remaining
trees. We've acquired a new 3-car garage with matching
house up on the ridge which is ruining the neighbor-
hood, the view & the eagles' nest. He had to tell me
about the very fancy job he'd had at microsoft as some
kind of genius but he'd given it all up to be more
natural. I covered my eyes with my hands, as though
the sun was too bright, so he wouldn't see my look,
which declared him a genuine idiot. I personally don't
know any Indians who'd give up a good job but I guess
we're already too natural. He wanted me to understand
a lot & so, though I just can't, I made the noises which
imitate comprehension. *Hey! that's too big a word! Get
back & be natural!* I was trying to remember my grocery
list while noticing that his new truck & matching boat
both matched his pearly baby blue eyes, which was quite
a fashion statement. My car is rusty beige to match my
tennis shoes. I don't know how to play tennis, however,
so I'd better call them sneakers, because, being Indian
(half-assed, but true) I'm definitely sneaky.
Mr. Wind Dancer is an Earth Steward, which seems to
mean that he stews about the earth a lot, but I'm not
sure this does the earth any good. He is also part of the

Native American theatre company, although I can't figure
out in what capacity—possibly prop boy.
I was very kind & didn't ask him to dance in honor
of his name because I could see it was all in his
mind & he probably couldn't have even told me which
direction the wind was blowing. I didn't scalp him either
because his hair wasn't very attractive. After I escaped,
still as unnatural as I can get in self-defense, I went
to the store, where I swear to you they had a plastic
container of jelly beans with a red & blue & yellow little war bonnet on top. I fell out laughing in the aisle &
the manager hustled up like the wind but I regained my
composure in time to avoid the cops. I just couldn't
afford to get those jelly beans for Mr. Wind Dancer,
which is a real shame. He could have glued that war
bonnet to the front of his truck. Now don't ask me what
I did buy, because it was all pretty unnatural, but I did
creep out, as close to the earth as I could get.

for Marie Annharte Baker

What Kills Me

is forcing myself to kill
the love I can feel for others
All the assassinations stare at me
with pitiful mouths
I cough despair
It's a long trail of blood
back to the moment
when survival meant
these icy knives
I know how to draw
so well
across the dirt

Your Beauty

is where I go to wash at dawn
your laughing eyes dry me
4 or 5 mountain ranges between us
Our snatched moments on other people's schedules
are bracelets I rattle as alone I lean into
a plane window to watch clouds bloom rainbows
rise up delicate birds
Over there is your old foxtail hairdo
Your sisters teasing you
Your hands creating mystery in midair
There's your sweet face wearing a baby bonnet
in the video
Up there is your honey voice making a big deal
about everything
Don't forget your lap & mine
becoming a park bench for some strange girl
to keep our minds off our broken hearts
Yeah & don't forget the months
I couldn't call your disconnected phone
that's stuck down there with those ant cars
tootling around with some flamingos
you left in Holland on your last tour
I tell the seat back that I don't know how
I'd stand it without you
but they just offer me some juice to shut me up
If I don't see you soon there's no telling
what I'll do

for Muriel

Hell Calls Me Up

Asks how I'm doing
I'm remembering terrible things in therapy
Well in that case I have to go now says Hell
mamadidsomethingi'mlittle
hide in the closet from her
Ne'er mind you can't do anything right
you filthy tramp
spread your legs like butter you'll get it now
Leave me the hell alone kid
Can't you shut up for one damn minute
She like to chase me
she like to beat me
break that stick on me
it help her feel better
You no good
worthless piece of trash
I'll teach you to run
from me   Come here & take your licking
I kill you mama
like you try to kill me
drown can't breathe
boiling medicine in my ear
choke me until I'm good
go inside my body
get out mama
If you don't stop sniveling
I'll beat the living daylights
out of you
Dark in here but I'm alive

Critics like to say art shouldn't be
this real
However if the purpose of art is to change the world
& it is
listen

Riding Up the Escalator

in a hurry
ahead of me
were some Black teenagers
laughing & talking
My very first thought was
Please live
Don't get shot or die from drugs
Same thing I pray
when I'm near young Indians
though I see them less often
When I watch white kids
my mind goes blank
with deadtired fear
Try to get away from them
without being noticed
This is the garbage that racism
makes of me
Can't even look at children
sing clear to their Spirits
Though this isn't the worst
of what's been done to us
in this late afternoon blessing of brief sunlight
it hung me out to rot on a barbed wire fence
I could hear my bones weep

Late Breakfast

When they put blue ice in her mind
when they took her name
burned her brain synapses
when they put her drooling in a chair
her hands like strangers
in her blue cotton pajama lap
when wet through the arms her
mind was lifted out with an electric pitchfork
pierced
when they stole her memory
traded her life for a rubber tongue depressor
when her tangled hair
wore the mark of their machines
her black eyes erased blank
when I saw what
they did to her
because she was depressed
I practiced smiling

for Pam

Volunteers of America for God
& Country Thrift Store

The bins groan muttering among themselves
making a bric-a-brac racket
old & used to it
I got my income tax all made out Ruby
she says standing next to an empty tyrolia bottle
of dusty red plastic tulips, one white rose, a pink
carnation & a baby blue bow
surrounded by a stack of round in square ashtrays
a shoe box full of clutch purses
kissing each other chartreuse brocade, pink leather
& lavender satin
while a white plastic dishpan of old stockings
& suspenders chatters on
A blue rose mattress has a faded sign
Keep Off This Means You
with 3 stuffed plush animals
a gray poodle, a black & yellow flowered thing
with red tongue sticking out, an orange cat missing
one eye and a tail
Shelves of white plastic straw purses
draw up contracts on one another
for elimination of so much shit
The gray wooden bins reveal mysterious chips
of former lovers in navy blue, hunter green
institutional tan & pure white
The bins of shoes talk to the girdles & bras
but not to the sofa cushions or children's overalls
Hats whisper red straw, white plastic turban, black velvet
with soiled edges

Toilet seat covers gossip with the belts & a rack
of various shades of brown corduroy jackets with
& without fake fur collars
The capri pants nod to a picture of the breck
girls smiling blandly forever but ignore
a shelf of satin-bowed heart-shaped candy boxes
relics of dead romance & bad chocolate
A green glitter candle stands by a blue bunny
offering therapeutic support
& a tiny bat to beat the used pillows
on aisle 3
Whatcha doin' honey?
I'm gonna write a poem about this place
Oh, will ya let me see it?
Sure
That's one thing I never
could do is write poetry some
people can I bet you're good at it
Thank you I mumble to a tin of unmatched buttons
& garters
This poem
sold as is
No refunds
No exchanges

Parsing Our Sentence

ONE YEAR

You'd had enough of me why couldn't I understand how
beautiful & vibrant she is
You couldn't help yourself why can't
I forgive you if only I'd try why am I refusing
to speak to you it's ridiculous nothing happened
it wasn't really a lie you always planned
to tell me you needed
the right moment
which was not
while I lay full of light in warm bathwater
renewed with promises of our life growing long
& tender as roses planted with both our hearts
outside our bedroom window
Is there another now who wrinkles
our sheets in my place
I avoid gossip mutual friends any place you might
appear with some ghost laughing beside you
She is
beautiful & vibrant still though nothing
happened between you two if nothing is defined
as two bodies naked sucking juices
Everything happened: I saw you cold selfish besotted
with my prior forgiveness
understanding I'd given until I was nothing
I happen to know
you did it on purpose
in just that way
so you could be free of me

Nothing was happening in our bed
as I remembered rape & rape weeping in your arms
as you bit back your fury that I was
more victim than you
stealing your center stage & right
my beauty a ghost
You hadn't had enough of me in months
I was slow untangling all the lies
that had kept me alive for years
Trying to forgive you
I don't understand when we were once
so beautiful & vibrant in each other's arms
It must be
that nothing happened

TWO YEARS

I'd had enough of violations you'd insist
were mere mistakes
As I ran toward forgiving myself
I couldn't help you
I saw that I'd used your pain to obscure my own
The dance shifted until I was the center of my grief
You were left alone with yours
Your love a response of leaf to light
I'd held your pain as mine
gave you every rain I knew
When I wanted my hands for myself
you rebelled in raging tantrums

your child once more denied
Under the water of your screaming
I held fast
believed your promises of change
Opened my arms as I never had
but I still wanted my own grief not yours
We rode in anguished circles shouting
You would not let me out

THREE YEARS

What I could not speak
you told everyone
a random crowd while I was gone
My rage was your puzzle as you insisted
that you were only trying to help
I knew you meant to stop me instead
I forgave you
opened my long shut legs
gave you the gift of light
Shaking in circles I didn't know
two bodies could make
Nothing before was like that dance
I'm afraid I won't
be able to do the steps again
All my meaning in your hands
you shrugged & gave me away
Trying to forgive my lies   you never understood
they were my breath

You remembered my other lovers with a clarity
as I forgot
You brushed yours aside as flies
They were the ghosts who laughed at us & wept
I've gone as far as I can go
carving silence to my need
This fresh coldness has no dance
The empty window where I dreamed our life
echoes as I ride past
The earth is dry, leaves & blossoms droop
The lie you held appears screaming
as it circles my weeping eyes
This dance of rain is for our vibrant beauty
now nothing now burnt hands no light

Hissing He Called Me a Witch

with scorn more slippery than I could stand
All I'd done was say *Excuse me*
when his oblivious spoiled son stood on my foot
& didn't get off
in a tone of voice
no white man stands from a woman like me
Next year I'll still want to punch his face
but I walked away with dignity
ignored him
as he told everyone at his table
in a loud voice I was meant to overhear
how rude I was
Someday I'll meet a real
witch & she'll help me teach him some
manners

for Celeste George

Your Hand the Hard Silk

bright bridge

my screaming cunt clutches

as our souls meet

dancing purple hyacinth tongues

Judas Hole

Back into reality
they said with a slam
in this cramped sight which sees 4 walls
& a locked door as real
I paced
Very boring what happens to trees
in reality
smooth straight white
They were hoping my mind would follow suit
Hallelujah for visions
which save us from situations like this
Painting the walls back into trees
sun   air   sparrows
I discovered with mischievous delight
in mathematical angles
a spot to the side of the door
wherein I could disappear from
the bald mean eye watching me
Sounds of rage interrupted my brief glee
Clanking open the big door
was a voice that shouted
This is not a game
This is serious business
Caught me in a strange white coat
that wrapped my hands around me like
throttled wings
or meat from the butcher

His needle stung me with barbed wire sleep
When I came to I pointed out
that reality
hasn't much to offer
an inquiring mind

in honor of Sheila Gilhooly

She Says My Dependency Needs

were never met
Standing near the flower shop in the rain
with no more than change to get home
I can't stand waiting for the bus anymore
Lope off over the wet streets prowling
as I did when I was 20 thinking
the next trick or drug or screwdriver
would dissolve this sharp garbage
caked in my fingers searching as I still am
for that dry warm shoulder to take me in
to a place with a big breakfast in the morning
& no questions

In the Morning I Comb

your juices from my hair

my fingers separate the snarled strands

traveled with light

my face smells of you

I don't wash

My Father Died at Nine

though he lived on to place himself in my mother
who named him rape
Born after long labor to almost die I beat
red to live fiercely
My father terrified of my cries
rowed to a distant sand where he would not
have to hear
Deaf he eats solemn meals exactly on time
his hearing aid turned off
dead for such a long time his husk
embraces me with dutiful arms
I'm the daughter who flew into his books
awkward crane listening with sharp ears
to nuances no one wants
to hear in their voices
I could be the seed of violence or rebirth
No path too narrow to test
Sound of a key rattling is my terror
labor of the wind

Rude as 2:29 A.M.

I can't sleep
You're here in my bed accusing me again of hurting
you because you thought I said I hated white people
but I didn't
say that
I said, *I don't have time*
to hate white folks
which offends you because it means you aren't
the center of the world as your whole life
has conspired to teach you
I'm sorry that I'm the first one to pierce
your ignorance
for both our sakes
but you're certainly not
the first white person of any age
to resent the clear white heat of my words
& attack me for them
You didn't want
to hear
anything I said
so you pumped up a response
that was your own myth
of what I did say
which is also not the first time
In fact that's the oldest story
of all the white history books
in our own land where we don't even
have a month to call our own
We face each other across an abyss of death

5 centuries of murder, rape & slavery
made this country
Being mad at me doesn't change the facts
Really it is
time now for all the white folks
to sit down & relax for a change
shut up
& listen
I just don't have time
to hate you
for more than a minute

for a young white man in my New Jersey audience

I Fly to You

to be soothed in the wings
of your Butch tenderness
hidden under fierceness necessary as mine
to ride your feather fingers & tongue
through an iris sky
We reach the moon in a moment
plunge through scarlet silk
careen into cascading coral
loll on lemon stars
wind our bodies around emerald
our breasts whisper cloudless blue
fall deeply coasting on indigo
bloom out lilac lace
Landing fat & filled
Your hands keeping me aloft
I fly for you

Sometimes I Can't Stand to Look

in your eyes you said with great love & tenderness
You're too much a mirror
We heal one another in short gasps
moments snatched from ordinary time
Going home you fell asleep across my lap
How carefully I cradled you
against the sharp turns in the road
watched your face go back
to the soft pictures of your early childhood
before the door started to
push open in the night

There's a Razor

that shreds us   We're on the side of living hand
to mouth one minute from homelessness
Seems like if you've never been here
you can't see us
We're debris in your eyes, diseased meat
time to call the kops
On the other side stroll the night
of the living mall shopper dead
they burble babble happy little rivers
of buy, buy, bought
So safe, so clean, so without a clue
Here's the street where you window shop
I'm here pan-handling with an eye peeled
our intersection   if I'm lucky
is your quarter
No words are a shower
no sympathetic glance is a hot meal
I ran away from hell
still running I don't know what home smells like
Anger rattles in my torn jeans
studs to mark my loneliness
if anybody gave a damn about me I'd sing
Can't trust anyone with more
I'm not going to be your happy patsy
taking the rap to clean up your mess
with your rope
I can kick ass
I can hum a mean tomorrow
Give me the quarter & shut the fuck up

for the young homeless people on Broadway

Folded Carefully

in a paper sack I return your $1.99 Dracula cape
which you claim I am holding hostage
but which I paid for
You've about sucked it dry
smugly satisfied when you can drive
me to audible sobs through the wire
It's an old trick I've used to get you off
my back   My weeping reassures you that my heart
is broken too   not as broken as yours
of course because it has to be
my fault we broke up
even though you tried to sleep with her
& that cape which has hung forgotten in my closet
is valuable property
Equal to the house we bought together
which you've kept
with vague promises of reimbursing me
if I agree to meet with you to argue
some more while I'm bleeding
so you can suck it up
This is yet another lie
Let this dried blood rest
there is nothing left for you in my teeth
You'll need this cape
to convince your next woman
to buy you an even better house
I'd like to strangle you or at least
convince you to stop calling to say we
could be reasonable if I'd just
try

A Dracula cape is an insane request
covering darkness for your heart which plans
to get me if you can
stuck on a stick of rage
This is bloody ridiculous
A rose light comes from my hand:
unclench your teeth let go

Gazing Out the Kitchen Window

during my break I watch
3 young children of the rich whites
playing on the beach
There is no one else around
this is Private Property
Squeals of delight float back to me
It is a delicate art to enjoy this fragment
of their pleasure
I have to scrape back all the ghosts
of slaughtered Indian children
& silence the Suquamish mothers & fathers
I have to believe in this carefully
contrived innocence
which may last until they're 60
or beyond their deaths
They're raised to know this is their beach
an ownership profoundly lacking in history
The crash of sun on waves
draws me back to work
They'll always have more time than I do
& do nothing much with it
They won't be servants
I can only know their joy
as a fragile shell
over my grief

for Marilyn Low

Worrying About How to Pay All My Bills

with one week left until the first
my mind a headache of amounts
due dates wondering where I could pick up an extra
job as I drive to polish silver & brass & copper
at the mansion larger than all the places I've rented
put together

A fawn leaps across the road

all the numbers fall into a heap where they belong

I see the Elder lady who winked & whispered

You read too many books honey

Sprouting I see the sky blue as beginning

sun glittering each new spring leaf

bold yellow swamp lilies

the deer watching me from a curve of emerald &

all the dancing birds breathe into my soul

In the Land of the Free

where they massacre the brave
imprison more people
than any other place on earth
where enormous wealth
accumulates from slave labor
where each of us
has been manipulated into believing poisonous lies
about ourselves, our needs
& our work
where art & poetry are dirty words
death is more common than bread for the poor
In the land of the free
white liberals write about how much
everyone else in other countries suffers
numb to our neighbors and families
When I go to Australia
speak of our homeless, our prison sentences
they are shocked unbelieving
Every city to which I have gone
has men & women & children
standing on freeway ramps or streets
with cardboard signs saying
Will Work For Food
in a country which is
called the breadbasket of the world
In the land of the free
my eyes still see
the slaughtered bodies of my ancestors
my back is raw with the memory of whips
my belly bitter with hunger

my mind aches & flails with lies
I grasp what I see
name it reality
Refuse to put on the emperor's clothes
pretend to be rich & happy drifting through movie stills
stoned out on drugs to disguise my despair
In the land of the free
I insist on wearing our chains
our mutilation
our shame

for Roseann Marble

Went Out

to get my mail in dozing afternoon sun

Heard plops on my shoulder

thought   *Ah it's raining again*

but as I moved toward home

noticed there were only those few

I glanced up

to see Eagle

circling

so I laughed out loud & lovely

standing in the road

with my head back & hair free

Giving thanks for that

very fertile blessing

for Wesley Thomas

His Beautifull Full-Blood Face

battered swollen with years of hatred
some of it scrawled by his own hand
My heart caught on his torn shirt sleeve
in the late day summer sun
as he passed head down
through crowds of yuppies, hippies & punks
who think they suffer
I know him
as I know myself
Who knows what tribe he's from
cousin or enemy
Doesn't matter anymore at all
I hurried to catch up with him
Have you had anything to eat?
No
I pressed some money into his hand
God Bless You, Sister
Went away my head hanging down
hearing the screams of a million americans
He'll only use that money to get drunk
I know
but he's part
of all that's left
of my family

in honor of Clyde Hall

I Lift the Pearl

of your pleasure into the light

of afternoon leaves with my

tongue hard to follow you

through drifting branches

The wind just catching

as a kingfisher

streaks blue into blue

Looks Like I Have That White Fang #2

in my neck again
another pale movie with a pretty
white boy in buckskins
communing with a wolf
& probably saving some Indian folks
from themselves
though at least
they look like they might actually
be Indians
instead of Jewish folks in max factor red #10
& braided wigs
which is how they did it in the good old days
This is a sincere sweet movie
by laladisney & I'd love to sincerely
sweetly say I'm glad
some Indian actors got some supporting roles
but I'm scrubbing out a white sink
for mr. white as I watch this ad on TV
& since I'm sick of weeping
all I feel like
is throwing up

for Lisa Bellear

This Whale Card

you send after two raw years of deepest silence
begins by saying I'm probably furious with you
for not writing or speaking
Late with assumptions
which flap our old air gasping
Angry for so long after you packed your clean
laundry / my work into matching luggage
& left our 8 years in 1 day
My rage a reason for you to escape
These words return say you're not good at writing
become stubborn when pressured
bursting from whales who possibly sing
or flee ambiguous as what you want from me
now
My anger beached itself in Oregon useless dead pain
bared teeth these whales suck prey through
I could write you a steamy plume of why
Trained at Marine World to rise to your bait
believed I was retired from grief you left
me swimming through
useless as the word *always* to mean love
you said so often or is it that you
think of me *sometimes even fondly*
as though singing were a new language
& the net of tricks we named love
has caught you unaware turning in circles
for red herring your nose against my fragile glass
wall house where you've never been
Never is another useless word which screams
Maybe whales have no purpose except as food for dogs

My new lover says whales have something
important to tell us
judging by your card of 2 whales possibly cavorting /
fighting for their lives / taking baths / spouting poetry /
glaring at the inevitability of your card /
which you thought I might like / it is true
This is a painter I admired when you & I were lovers /
pain / before I preferred my own colors
You tell me about your job with computers
Life here is fine
I consider writing you an unsigned postcard saying
Define *fine*
Soon you'll be on vacation in the same place where
I'll go to a workshop with my typewriter /
pain / but I'll still swim
You'll be with Lesbian wife & child
your loving patriarchal whale song
untouched by the harpoon of feminism
You end with the words, *Say hi to J*
She hates you as you've felt
not simply as the woman I couldn't give up
or as former lover logged in photo albums
she hates you / for / me
how could I /
pain / hate you despite this long stabbing separation
when there were not enough fish for us both
After you walked out /
pain / scenes between us were common as herring
red battles waged in the teeth of embarrassed friends
angry new lovers / stunned passersby

You sign yourself   *love*
I amend my postcard: Define *love*
Even fondly I don't understand the songs
of whales or you
A card with such a boring faded print would be burned
if written by anyone else
I crumple & smooth & recrumple my fingers touch
your writing as though I could feel your heart
You still insist on breaking the water of my need
Finally abandoning obsession only
to find I'm frequently given
what I've so desperately wanted
when I can no longer swim in it
I wanted you
in some capacity: memory / floodlight / whale
teeth to slip through / family
I gave you up / tired of waiting for you to go away
Get off this beach
You're dead gray fish in my mailbox
Your words rip / Nostalgia is a disease which smells
a quiet killer   I can't do tricks
must have open sea   Why
did you write
why did you leave
don't say you care / pain / no more herring for you
I'm not furious
You're no longer the keeper of my feelings
Or I'm more furious than a letter could hold
Stubbornly I won't tell you I'm fine
because I'm still not & perhaps will not

ever heal from your amputation of love that word
like prey / which circles me a flyer about whale watching
from a boat with no return address / I'm fighting
for my life I'm not good at writing any
of this / you won't see it until the phantom
pain in my arms is silent
My darling I am not furious I wept with joy
to see your writing   which I'll never admit
Went down to the water to remember how
we were one motion in such tender light
Wept with a gash in my throat
where I'm too stubborn to recover from your teeth
The whale you were lives on in my body
I feed her when no one is looking
though it is clear / pain / we cannot
fit each other ever again
& I admit I have nothing I can say to you
that would not beach itself to die
This silence
as great as a sea in which we both have drowned
what I sang to you
useless
with no place to go

for Peter, my first woman lover

Your Gentleness Sweeps

across my plain

skin like tumbleweeds

Your fingers are afternoon rain

drifting light

You're hungry wind

your mouth tender as jack rabbit eyes

blooms quickly spring

I open myself beside you

in slow motion trance

We sprout blue camas

Night Watch Me Closely

I'm invisible turn away ticking
You won't find us in anthologies of american poets
We forgot to sign that treaty
Everybody likes to read the whites writing myths of us
Us telling about us is too hard
Pouting she tells me how she cried & cried
after reading *Bury My Heart at Wounded Knee*
I coughed   looked away   disappeared
certain not to comfort her
These expectations a matter of course
like too tight shoes
Veering coarse my words are spittle
See them evaporate on the sidewalk sputtering
near your sneakers as you patrol reality with a stick
beating back our tears
I sniff the books rolling out in which we're footnotes
walking away into a hollywood sunset
where the west was won
in a stacked poker game of cheats
Hey I'm not screaming since you're not listening
This, our pulse   We are the heart of your lives
your lies
Caretakers of what you presume to own
Laughing I'm a puff of smoke signaling
in some cowbullshit movie
running fast forward
Being Indian is being a surrealist
You won't find us in your local library stoic & strong
except in volumes of defeat speeches
they call our literature

Millions
of dead
are in my voice
Rerun that through the tape of your mind
Look for them as a matter of keening necessity
Cry Now   as you erase these
mean angry words with whitewash
The spirits won't hear
I'm a ghost dancing with hands on fire

Heaven Hill

You don't know how many times, my Turtle Gal, you've
said, *I love you sweetie,* with a catch in your voice that
has saved my sanity   You don't know how many times
I've talked about your stories, how many nights cryin'
at the ends of my rope I've thought of your kind eyes,
remembered all the times your raucous laughter has
burst the skin of racism or whatever nonsense was
pounding me down   Never told you that I agree to
go to conferences I'm not interested in because they
mention that you'll be there   I sleep with your books
near my bed, have kept every letter, card & valentine
you've ever sent   When death creeps close whispering
my song, it's your quick warm hands & heart who help
me chase that colonizer out   You don't know all
the letters my spirit has written you, those who never
traveled down a pen   You don't remember a blue
basket day when I caught you & Glorita grinning at me
in front of brilliant waves, a photo that keeps my desk
anchored in this world   Don't know how many times
I've prayed for your health, for your lover to come to
her senses   You don't know how many times I talk
to you as I wash dishes or vacuum some job's floors
Now you do

for Beth

Simplicity

Even in metaphor, the abstract world of crafted writing,
I realize, 35,000 feet away from the earth, that I carry
them, I speak inside their shadows, though we are not
speaking to each other. As I remembered brutally in
therapy, the fragments joining at last, so that I knew the
truth, I said, *It was a sound, a feeling as though train cars*
were joined in me, that specific loud slamming thwack.
I've heard that sound a few times but it comes from
my father who was a hobo for 7 years before he met
my mother. I'm using his life to describe my feelings
about what my mother did. I protested in the electric
memory chair that I didn't want to remember. She
reassured me that I didn't have to, for I'd already
survived it. Fragments tormented me. Terrified of water
in my face, avoiding showers for days, terrified of hands
near my throat, careful to push away lovers' hands &
warn them. I was tying my sneakers when I had a full
body orgasm because a baby was being diapered on TV.
A memory which continues to arouse & nauseate me.
My mother was alone, working as a secretary. Daddy
had taken off. Her mother wouldn't help. The whole
world was still ripped open from the war. At night,
tired from her job, she bathed me, played with my
genitals, smashed my face in the water, grabbed my
throat, ripped with catholic guilt, despair, disgust, in a
rage that my father had swollen her up with me & left.
No one wants to believe me. I'm not supposed to be
alive if it really happened. I can't remind her of this
or any of it. This is my revolting secret, my sexual
revulsion for women who look like her, matronly,

big-breasted, pale, conventional. It is not accidental
that both of my long-term therapists have this
appearance. I've saved myself from the devastating
complications of desiring my shrink, a contradiction
I'm incapable of surviving.

It is simple. I understand her hatred of me. Trapped
with the burden of my care, none of the romantic
fantasies she concocted (& still yearns for) around my
father ever possible, she was poor & demented with
shame & need & loneliness. I can imagine my own
hands around an infant's throat, especially an infant
terrified of me, screaming. Never forgotten being
terrified of my mother, lying still & frozen in a harsh,
white starched dress with tiny flocked red hearts.
Dressed like a doll she could pretend she loved. Every
expert says that I could not remember that moment.
I was wondering if I would live or die, bracing myself.
I didn't remember why I was so frightened. Now I
know. I want to go on being split from this terror.
Return to being crazy, imagining things. But I've heard
that sound. It's final. So many mysteries lie still
& revealed.

I wasn't an abortion because she was catholic & scared.
I wasn't a sudden infant death baby for the same reason.
I grew up despised, feared, resented, beaten. She began
telling me I was just like my crazy grandfather before I
talked. It's easier for both of us if I'll be crazy. *I don't
ever have to see her again or talk to her, do I?*
No.

There is a baby screaming who won't be consoled.

I'm shaking to know that the brainwashing of the
catholic church, the church which I hate with a burning
passion for destroying my life in so many ways, for its
long history of genocide, that brainwashing saved my
physical life as a baby.
How can I stop myself from hating women who love
their mothers or mothers who love their daughters?
It was so simple. This is why I've spent my life trying
to kill myself so that I would not know.
Nauseous again as I was throughout my childhood
when my mother touched me, very rarely, always in
public. I don't call beatings (frequent & private) touch.
I've been repulsed by her always, deeply ashamed of it.
Thought I loved her passionately. It was not love, I was
begging to live by adoring her in the manner which she
demanded. Bribing her, coddling her, spoiling her, lying
every hour of our mutual torture. She doesn't know how
many nuthouses there have been. This is murder to
write. I thought I was protecting her but I was
protecting myself. I wouldn't give her the satisfaction.
My mother was the first white person who hated me.
It's no wonder I am who I am.
Simple.

*for Marilyn Low, whose clear light of friendship
made these words possible*

This Weekend Butch

comes up to me in the bar
She thinks she's so
fine she gives me a headache
She's busy tellin' me how wonderful
she's gonna make my life if I just
go home with her tonight
which I don't do without
charging since strangers
are tricks
She was pretty
damn tricky leanin' into me
like she thought she could please me
& I didn't have a hanky
anywhere in sight
I knew with my old whore's nose
that she dresses up like this to cruise
but wears a skirt to work
She even had discreet little matching
holes in her ears
I didn't wanna see her next weekend
in a black lace bustier
so I smiled purring
Sorry baby
I only
like my Butches
daily

for Viv & Lyn

Looking Through a Picture

book of women we found Margo St. James
founder of COYOTE
What's that? she said her voice ringing
Clearly I was at a loss
A group of prostitutes who have
banded together to give one another strength
to fight their legal oppression
What's a prostitute? she stumbled over the word
My throat caught
9 is too young to know
& yet I'm always honest with her
A woman who goes with men to get money
What for?
(Yes my whole body whispered
What For?)
Well, it's not a pleasant subject
They have sex with men for money
How disgusting she said
turning the page, my heart, my memories
my own sacred place
where I too
once paid dues
Earlier a male acquaintance at a restaurant
had offered to take care of something for me
I heard take care of me   to take something from me
I announced from the door
No one takes care of me but myself
My pride stirred clearly with old anger
past debts   past sperm   passing time
Looking through to myself in her clear just-9 eyes

my love now given to women
how sacred
I hold myself whispering
I'm out of that book
no longer at a loss

When You Were Four

your mother left without
notice you woke up & running
to her bed learned to howl
You weep telling me this
I weep listening
I couldn't tell you then
but I can now
When I was 4 my mother
threw out my lamb
saying I was too old for toys
I was afraid to howl
then & these tears now
are your gift to me at 4
who didn't have a mother
I could trust
She knew the lamb
was my only friend
which enraged her
She needed me to be as poor
as she thought she was
No small thing your mother gone
without a word
My 4 comforts yours
Your mother came back
but I know it was never the same
We've shaped ourselves from loss
Let's make a place where our grief is safe
This is no small task

for Margaret Sloan-Hunter

Marti's Poem

I remember my cousin
telling me they'd had some girl
down by the railroad tracks
When they left they thought
she was dead
but they weren't sure
Gang rape white trash girl nobody cares
disposable dixie cup
raised to please men to death
didn't have a moment
to say a prayer
I keep thinking & thinking
of her mama
It was almost like they'd run over a dog
& didn't bother to stop to see
if they'd killed it

State troopers report a DRT
out by the old side track
Information is sought on identity
of the victim
a white female approximately 18–20 years
brown hair about 5'4" 110 pounds
wearing a pink flowered cotton dress
shoes & purse missing

DRT *is cop slang for "Dead Right There"*

At Another Writers' Conference

I should have missed
to work on the weeds in my garden
there's some guy upstairs
with a fancy computer
which he has programmed
for what he calls
Interactive Poetry
He tried to show it to me
& I said without realizing
my rudeness
But the text is boring!
It was
Pedestrian language, clichés
He was so interested in his technology
that he forgot to say
anything
Of course, I saw his empty
spirit & glazed eyes
knew he doesn't have
anything to say
I felt sorry for him
briefly

for Kathe McKnight

Rant in the Bloody Face of It

I didn't know you planned to suck a gun
with your soft lips
I didn't ever get to kiss
It was fucked up
There ain't enough
workin' class Butches
in this narrow world
You're the first ones they kill
& you had to go
do that
to yourself
It wasn't noble
or necessary
I'd give anything
to be able to hit you over the head
with an iron fryin' pan
right now
for being so dumb
because it'd mean
you were still
alive

For the Trees

The buzz saw cuts out my heart
leaves stumps tombstones
goes through my bones changing blood to sap
I feel my flesh give way   crack of death
The heavy satisfaction of the logger who cuts
down life in its prime
The uncle who once raped me regularly
came to this country as a logger
Don't have to know english to slash
Comes natural
For a moment the buzz saw stops
air breathes a sigh of relief
I was so proud & happy the day the dog & I found
all their yellow plastic ribbons saying execute
this one & this
Here is the road through the heart of our crushed ferns
splinters, shards of bark, our deep ridges of bulldozer
Here is where we sweat & laugh our hands
sticky as butchers'
I removed every yellow ribbon in the forest
stuffing them greedily into my pocket sure
that I was delaying them for weeks
Only a few days passed
They put up large angry signs every few feet
saying *No Trespassing*
Every day they come insistent on cutting
I sit in my studio unable to work
on paper that was once a tree
My hands sticky with fear
I burn a red candle of love & sorrow & death

I want to use
the stolen yellow ribbons to make
something that will stop clearcutting
Silver graveyards where nothing grows for years & years
unwanted wood rotting & choking the earth
Too barren even for bugs
When I saw my first clearcut I fell down
weeping couldn't get my breath
screamed anger for the waste
threw rocks at passing trucks
with logs stabbed together
bleeding bark down the road
No one
tills a clearcut for food or flowers
no animals graze
The silence stares up into the sky
Wind comes through a knife saying
I'm raped I do not move I'm impaled I'm avoided
Eyes seek the green ribbon of the false scenic root
Smokey the Bear protects the lumber industry's crop
Fire is not profitable
Do you wonder
when I obsessively reuse scraps of paper
write on the backs of movie listings, car wash fliers,
restaurant placemats, bill envelopes, reading posters
Every paper is a green leaf, root, branch, swirl of grain
a heart of life now dead
Do you wonder that I burn to get warm
with downed branches, paper trash
the neighbors' discarded xmess trees

Abundance seems to stupify
I've been jumpy all week as they cut
Afraid that they would slip & get me
Afraid that when I can go back in the woods
I won't be able to stand the gore
Afraid that I am the one
who has broken the law
The day I took the yellow ribbons off
I thought of sneaking back that night
to dig up some of the smaller trees to plant here
No one "logs" a front yard
But we were too tired   I thought
I had plenty of time
All week they have been crying out to me
The yellow ribbons mock me, a mask of war
They still believe they have to conquer
& are different from the desk jockeys
who use reams & reams of paper
to say not much
The day I removed their yellow brands
I got lost in the woods
couldn't find the trail out again
I laughed so hard at myself
My dog was the one who led me back to the road
I am
part of the plundering & raping
accustomed to warm fires in winter all day
fresh vegetables in January, someone else to bring water
I am the very person who breaks
my heart open with sap

I couldn't live simply in the gentle ways of my ancestors
I don't want to spend all day
gathering food
preparing it
making clothing against the cold
I like to draw my visions with prisma colors
& paints from a tube
Use fountain pens, books, stereo
electric blanket on frosty nights
I'm as much to blame as the buzz saw
which tears my ears
I didn't start out
to see myself reflected in its blade
This was going
to be a passionate plea for an end to logging
Especially across the road from me
The trouble with writing is that you end up
being cut by the truth
Sorrow turns to laughter at the self
who would claim innocence
The task I'm left
is learning to live more simply
with less waste
resisting more firmly
fads for more things
even from the wildlife protection catalogue
or the feminist bookstore
Remember now that my great-great-grandmother lived
her entire life without reading a book
or going to market for vegetables

How can I learn to step as softly as she did
I begin using only cotton rag paper to draw
gather more downed wood instead
of buying a cord already split
Give attention to my laziness
The buzz saw eats the edge
of my ears as I write
close enough to kill

Dance for Me

like a manchurian crane

black legs against

fierce snow

I'll leave bundles

of your favorite foods

I Was Falling Wet Red

leaves across my face
Only the moon would hold me
as I dug up my 11-year garden in the wind
She decided I was her enemy
would not open my love
roses on her floor
her silence ice
I asked for deer to bless me through tears
they came to the road's edge
hooves deep in gold
This is my season of loss
harvest killed in frost
How I kept breathing
after she felled me
is an art of new mulch
Not a shallow grave
our love burns in the storm
My lights go out
power fails
In the deep darkness
snowflakes form inside glass
I look for a match   a lantern
a voice singing me on
She was the way I knew
home of my words
she was a sky of stars more than she dreamt
One survives
but here
the wound

for GJJY

Why Indian Unemployment is *So* High

People just can't seem to understand
there are just some things Indians aren't any good at
For instance, serial killing
We just don't have
a Jeffrey Dahmer or Ted Bundy
That's a white folks' forte
They're really good at murder
but don't test for it in their IQ races
Indians are no damn good at double talk
If we say we'll do something we really do
do it
eventually
We expect likewise but continuous treaty violations
have shown us we just
don't get it
They say everything they do is because of jesus
I must say he seems to be a twisted dude
Indian giver is a phrase they made up
they do that best of all
If the baby is sick or Grandma fell over & hurt her hip
we won't get to work on time
Since nobody wants us & most of us
have no money or power (in the white world)
trauma happens to us
a lot
Bosses just get sick of hearing about it
We *are* good at dancing & singing but so far
no business who has called a powwow
has asked us to come along & cheer things up

Most of us can cook on nothing
better than jesus
but rich folks don't like the taste
We're excellent philosophers rambling on into the night
about the meanings of life
(you'll notice that definite plural)
but since most universities don't *like* our meanings
if you take my meaning
they don't hire us to teach at $40,000 a year
They'd rather pay some white guy
who showed up one summer
passed around booze bucks
to tell them what we think
'Course nobody actually told him
anything important
because he wasn't related
That's our other problem
We like to live together
sometimes 10 or 11 or more of us
at once & it makes some people real scared
that we like each other so much
'cause some of us may not be blood kin
which means you could feed anybody
who was hungry for free
which is so scary they made it against the law
unless you're a church
& harassing people about jesus
The main things Indians
are good at are love & forgiveness

which have absolutely no market value
which is why we haven't formulated our
immigration policy along more appropriate lines
My suggestion for alleviating this serious crime
is for all the mean white folks
& everybody who wants to act like that
to leave
We'll have lots of work then
cleaning up this big old mess

for Barbara Cameron Nation Shield

She Didn't Want

me to touch her in the accident of close coach seating
her pale body jerking away
from my red leg or jacket edge
in the bitterness of a 5-hour cross-country flight
My feet swollen in my boots
her mouth so prim you could fit it in a soda bottle cap
tight her irritation a repeating slap
First I was angry then ashamed then I pitied her
whose life snaps shut like her smooth leather handbag
on the crumpled white tissue she sniffed in
I thought about how little she has
entombed in heavy gold jewelry
discreet cake of lady make-up
boring navy dress & matching shoes
shiny stockings pinching the backs of her knees
hair perfect as her timid silence is a roar
her unhappiness shouting from her stiff lap
as she deferred to her arrogant husband
whose body treated her with a disdain
sharp as the one she directed at me
I wanted to take
her in my arms comforting
that shell whose soul lives so far out in nowhere
Her inhumanity to herself astounding cold
even as she angrily dodged my savage elbow again
I could imagine stroking her expensively shorn hair
a dry cracked
sound of her tears

in honor of Mab Segrest

Bête Noire Mama

My black beast of secret hatred bland surface
of dresses sewn for easter
homemade bread whose yeast kept me ill
sunday mass where I prayed fervently
for no more beatings
Spore growing in me
until I believed her accusations
names vile as the history of the church she adores
All my deaths rose from her song
I strangled her
when I was 15
as she had choked me
at 3 months & 5 months & 10
Both of us failures with not enough nerve
Pink lambs of denial erase these sacrifices
Years I've pretended nice for her sake
created faces dressed for any occasion
a self exploding like mold
This was my penance
I declare myself absolved of the sin
of being born
I tie you mama to your black beast
Send you howling out of my heart
Careen around now in some other prison
I've taken my keys away

Riding in Your Sidekick

I slide my hand along your thighs
my fingers thrill
to the line of your boxers
under your levis
Suddenly you're standing beside me
near our bed
your T-shirt & boxers wet
with my cunt juice
& your delicious
I-got-what-I-wanted
grin
your hand patting my ass
which still
shivers

Nightmare I Turn You

into a shimmering black satin steed who speeds
me away from their snarling wire
your neck damp   ears back   tail lashing
leaving clumps of turf cut through
My raped open legs clench your strong flanks
as we gallop into daylight
Waking me up your hooves are seeds of sleep
Arms embracing your fast spin
my fingers wring peace from your mane
Nightmare I flip you into a wide woods
where they have not been
Light comes through the branches
like family
with a tenderness I invent
from the dead leaves of their pain
I ride you   ride you   turn you
until you
leave

Corrugated

Here are the boxes of your stuff saying
Good-bye we've had it with you
I could kick them
get them wet with tears
you'd still go
Your eyes confused it's the one thing
you know for sure   *Good-bye*
I'm not sweet enough
I slam the door to keep from seeing them
throwing you in the street
I don't come home
something about boxes & how they look away from me
don't meet my eyes or expectations
how they're numb & read murder mysteries
would do anything to get me to leave them alone
It's that uniform dull color
with cigarettes hanging out
those boxes which say gilbey's gin
acme beer   almaden chablis
The boxes tell me that you once wanted me
but we won't go into that
boxes prefer the tidiness of silence
They judge my anger
inform me I'm crazy which I've heard before
& ignore
Here we are all packed up ready to go
I won't remember the first time we kissed
wasn't sunny we weren't on the golden gate
merry-go-round & I wasn't laughing

We didn't stay up all night making love
in a borrowed bed
It's all packed up ready to sit in a damp garage
warping

A Valentine

to the heron huddled in cold rain

whose soft dark ash gray shape

with head tucked

opened my heart

like lace

for Pat

I Have Three Names

ANNA   There is no scrapbook of smiling faces for
the years 1965 & 1966. Those are some of the hours,
bars across all the windows, when I learned that sanity
is balancing a checkbook, holding a job & keeping a
grocery list. *Where are you now, Anna?* Are you still
washing his dishes, the husband who committed you
because you asked for a divorce? I see you in my
bathwater screaming as they dragged you down the hall
to shock treatment. You were the only one who resisted
them. Passionate, you were so alive & then you were
not as much anymore. Your black eyes became hidden,
I saw the ax fall, I heard the dagger of your voice. *Anna
where are you?* I need to know you survived, that you
broke his dishes over his head. Are you locked up again
and again? Where are we? I can't forget. The therapists
keep telling me that you're not important, that was a
bad time best forgotten, but you are sitting here on my
hands. You want a voice & my throat is full of tears.
They belong to you. *Anna where are you? Where am I?*
Now they say I am sane. I've forgotten the language
I created whole, not even a scrap remains. Where are
the satiric collages about power that I made with bits
of hoarded candy wrappers, tinfoil, jokers & kings of
hearts smuggled from card decks with money I saved
for a bottle of glue? There were no art supplies at napa
state hospital. They said you and I were dangers to
ourselves and others. They said I was chronic, which
means I wasn't supposed to ever be able to write this
& I can't. How can I bring your screams, which cut
through linoleum, glass, plastic chairs, oak doors,

thorazine—how can I bring you alive & screaming
onto this paper? How can I make it against the law
for a husband to commit his wife? How can I change
what they did to your red red mind, your hot coffee
tongue, your laughter that I didn't hear that often? Anna
come back here, live with me, I won't ever lock you up.
I'll help you find work & words, a place to live, friends.
Anna it was so unnecessary, but I didn't know that
then. Every morning they fried you. You'd come back
babbling like an egg. Shots ring out in the night. I hope
someone has murdered your husband. Your black eyes
& hair & gold skin woke me up. *Are you still alive?* Are
you locked up? You went away. We were not allowed to
write to you. The rules say psychiatric prisoners cannot
communicate with released ones. They say we might
cause you a relapse. We are dangerous to ourselves,
Anna. We are dangerous to others. Are you still
dangerous? I'm careful to conceal my dangerousness.
No, don't ever strap me to a table or a bed again or lock
me in a room with no clothes no blanket don't rape me
with a towel stuffed in my mouth help me no more with
stelazine & thorazine. They were a danger to us, Anna.
They destroyed you. I pretend I am not destroyed, in
order to be accepted & safe but I have a dead language
stolen, I have drawings I'm afraid to do. My confiscated
art was proof of my mental incapacity. I'm not allowed
to see the files they kept on me, over a yard thick by
the time I escaped. It's against the rules for me to have
my drawings back. *How could I dare draw again?* We are
dangerous to the files. Your screams are not recorded

in them. Did it say, *Patient again difficult upon receipt of electroshock; we recommend higher doses of drugs?* The rape they did, the rape they do. The therapists I went to later did not want to talk about napa. They wanted to talk about my mother, who never tried to electrocute my mind, force tranquilizers on me or tie me to a bed naked, though she did commit me. The damage done to the damaged is worse. The moon is full of us tonight. Anna this is our moon we were crazed. Are we still crazed but better at lying? I hear a siren. *Who are they locking up now?* Anna please get out of my shoulders. I want to hold you. They wouldn't let me. I saved your breakfast those mornings but you drooled didn't know me you didn't know Anna. Hours and hours later you would slowly rise out of the death you would look confused. Anna they ruined your mind. They helped it right out of existence. After 10 shocks you said, *I am going to tell them that I feel much better. I do not want a divorce, I was mistaken, I want to go home to my husband.* I wanted to scream / didn't / having been there so long / I knew better. I see myself throwing a table through the windows. Was that someone else? So drugged we all became one pulse of sorrow. Did I throw the table through the window because you went back there to the home where he locked you in? *Anna are you free yet?* Am I? The main part of pretending to be sane is not talking ever about when you weren't or when they said you weren't but I can't tell the difference myself. I hide who I am. Sometimes I can balance my checkbook. I don't scream often. My throat is clogged. Am I sane,

Anna? What do these tears mean to you? Do your
children look at you strangely & wonder if you'll get
like that again? Can you remember the past? Did he kill
you enough to keep you? They couldn't give me shock
because I was born with a heart defect & would have
died. The nurses hated me because they couldn't do
that. They like to do it. They did other things to me
instead. I still have a very strong bladder. 10 or more
hours strapped down refusing to be humiliated in my
own urine. They hated my pride. They hated yours.
Pride in a woman is a sin, Anna. They punish it.
Were we crazy then? I felt you in me. I loved you,
I hated your husband, I worried about what happened
to you. I have never forgotten you. Is that crazy? I don't
remember your last name because it was his. Your soft
full red lips, your probing eyes, your arched nose.
How small you were, thin with bony wrists. *Anna
where are you?*

PAM   You told me very funny stories of your
failed attempts to kill yourself. Your mother worked in
the sewing sweatshops of Chinatown where the tourists
bought tin cable cars & ashtrays with blonde nudes.
Your hunger. A father who beat you & beat you & beat
you & beat you & you didn't die. The hospital thought
you were crazy to want to kill yourself when you were
so young. As young as I. You couldn't get a job. What
you knew was the back streets of Chinatown, your
family in one room. Once we pretended we were
american cheese melting & covering the whole world.

You too saw the blue streaks cure. The jolt you and jangle you and wipe you out cure. It was supposed to cure your depression. They did it 32 times. You were still depressed. Still did not want to live. They didn't talk about poverty or racism at the state hospital. It was all our fault. They decided finally that you were cured. You had not changed the whole time I was with you. They put you to work in a winery picking grapes. Because I was sleeping with a technician who would smuggle letters for me, we wrote to one another for a while. You liked living in the valley with the vines and the hills and the sun and all that room. *Where are you, Pam?* You showed me books I'd never seen before. You taught me some patience, some silence. You did not scream on the way. You were carved of wood. It must have seemed just like a beating from your father. Your long beautiful black hair tied back in a rag. They wanted to cut it off, as they had done mine, because it was in the way when they shocked you, but that was your only resistance to them. A quiet *No,* they respected as they respected none of us. I wanted the mystery of your power. Are you awake yet? Are you still picking grapes? I was in love with you & was afraid to tell you. When I try to write about you I become wooden. Did the grapes heal you? Were we crazy? Did my lover drink wine tonight that you made?

TERRY   Silk dove they separated us because they caught us holding one another. You taught me how to slice my arms with razors, bartered with kisses from the

men who were on the drunk ward. Once you took your
psychiatrist, a friend of your psychologist father (who
was told everything you said), a bowl of your blood,
which repulsed him. I thought it very powerfully
symbolic since they want to drain us that way. Strip
us of memory pain the incomprehensibility of everything
they want us to *Fit In*. Maybe if we cut off our arms
we will. The elusive glamour of scars. In public I wear
long sleeves, tired of lying or explaining my scars. They
were our joint ritual of love. I couldn't feel the cuts
mired in so much thorazine. No feeling at all. I watched
the gush of blood with an artist's fascination for the
brilliant rubies of it splattering into the toilet swirling
& pooling in the water going pink. Careful to always
cut myself over the toilet so as not to get caught. We
pulled our black regulation cardigan sweaters down over
the open lips of our despair. When they found out, they
shipped you to an isolation cell on the violent ward,
where the screams would keep you awake even through
a haze of more drugs. Your father thought there was
something wrong with you because you weren't happy
& refused to date. A mental hospital where he worked is
certainly the only cure for that. My scalp crawls with
your father, chills running up my head—hard to be
happy with a man like that on your neck. We were in
love, wrote letters they confiscated, our love even more
proof that we were diseased. Our kisses met with
increased doses, separate wards, lockdown, not allowed
to see one another or speak. Your father pulled you out
of there. We wrote secret letters for a year or so later

and then you joined a guru commune & I knew I'd
never hold you naked in my arms or make the love
we needed for our scars. I wanted us to stop cutting
ourselves but we went on. Up against a razor I can't go
any deeper the bars are up I can't remember any more.

Cherishing My Heart

snared in hands of hatred
who maul me for one excuse or another
Weary of figuring out whys & wherefores
Looking for a place to hide
in a land stripped of all we love
Left on this concrete desert of trees dying
in straight rows of shame
Bitter with grit of stares, comments   Afraid
This war was lost before I was born
Stupid naked fool in a sandstorm
bruises all mine at night when I huddle
praying for Creation to guide me through these knives
they call career   publishing
performance   academic acceptance
I piss on it
Too large for syphilization
Too angry for receptions with raw carrots
Nothing will change my sharp spirit
tone down my raving tongue
sole weapon
in these battles where all the rules
were made up without my consent
This is a parched white world
owned   operated   signed   sealed
Lucky to be alive I hurt too much to be brave
Old & tired I'm going for a walk with the sea
who's never asked a stupid question   insulted me
demanded I fix her or begged for an interview
Going off with waves
where I move clear

For Stephen

Though we've been in the same canoe
we weren't rowing together
waves caught us at different dawns
Each of us memorized another oar of denial
smiling a wide grimace of similar teeth
to hide our confused smothered grief
I rode anger until my thighs were bruised
you avoided it until your hands can't get warm
Shut off we've reduced ourselves
to broken bones of dreams
for the convenience of others
We've been doormats   verbal punching bags   failures
Children of two who hate each other
themselves   & us
Rename their hate
true love
until the survival of our tenderness is a miracle
Brother in speaking with me at last
over a long tow rope of silent terror
you give me this great gift
of knowing it wasn't all in my mind
Not crazy you & I are family
though none of the others is
Come from the same screeching storm
we bear witness
to a destination with a deep calm cove
place where our fingers stretch out
feel the light

My Nickname is Miz FireEngine

My Butch
always
takes me to such nice
places when I spread my legs for her
down into burgundy velvet   shooting out silver
floating on a sea of pink rose petals
electric with blue light   colors with no name on earth
I always
make a lot
of noise in appreciation
but sometimes I have to keep it low
'cause all her roommates
are home trying to watch a show
or we're in somebody else's place
& they don't do it loud
or my niece & nephew are in the next room
You know all about that being polite & decent routine
So one time when I was way out
there in the stars
she had me trembling & weeping in pure light
I heard a fire engine coming down
the street so I thought *Great*
I can just let go now 'cause nobody will hear me
but do you know
her roommates can't stop teasing me
they say
Girl you're louder than a doggoddamn
red fire engine

Gwennie

is a funny black squat dog with a big head
who you could call ugly
but we don't
who was so glad to see me
that all the airports & strangers
fried up to nothing
So when I fell asleep on the couch
& she sprawled on my belly
her sweet weight
tamed my racing heart

for Craig Womack

I Call

your name in the wind's silence   I stand in the place
where we promised a life together   You left town early
Said you were sorry for using me   Which leaf curled
you dark   your back turned   your voice a scraping
wire   I opened my windows to breathe your air
You broke panes of glass across my bed   Don't ask
how I am as though we were friends & this dying light
a stranger's gift   I call your name   The wind folds
it back   a bit of debris   I call your name erasing you
I rake my hair   your twigs fly off   Whatever words
you spoke were lies   You have to live with your lips
I've gone for a walk my beauty blowing around me
The storm recedes   You could see sun breaking
through the rainbows in my lashes if you had courage
I glance backward   You're a fallen tree sprouting ferns
I wrap myself in light

In the Ferry Ladies' Room

an 11-year-old girl
with no breasts yet
carefully applied mascara & blusher to her face
as I washed my hands I thought of you
Your acid comment on all those
who have benefited from our work
while trashing us
The child's girlfriend copied her
Their mothers don't know
as mine didn't
sent them out shopping in cotton
summer dresses with some
absurd belief in innocence
I went up on the sun deck
to paint my toenails coppersilk red
a habit as non-feminist as any
but one, like your cigarettes
I can't give up
even though innumerable sincere
women have informed me that my nails can't breathe
I'm thinking about how little air we have
how those girls shouldn't disturb me & do
shouldn't increase my sense that our work
hasn't gone anywhere near to what is needed
shouldn't make me want to weep in the sun
because their faces
are already more important
than their minds

for Robin Morgan

I Scar Myself

arms deep in this tunnel where I've buried children
I was
My skin opens for them ripping burning erupting
stolen scalpels enter howling
You say   *Don't be afraid*
This is how you survived
They carry fragments of your life
which you must embrace if you are to heal
All of them screaming at once boiling
fury of pain enters my fingers see red
see red
Slash is the currency of breath someone
wants to finish this off
entomb them again for good
Leave that old ma to lie mournfully *I did the best*
I could   She was such a difficult child
beatings   hunger   rape   weeks of silence hide
in the letters for her "best"
Him to say   *Nothing*
ever happened she lied
disgusting lies she just wanted
to make trouble for me
Arms raw blistered with wounds
On fire with memories I scar myself
to stay alive

for Pat

Only a Small Patch of Her Hair

& her feet have survived unburnt his attack
on her with gasoline
& match
He was mad at her
about something
She lies unconscious a blur of
unimaginable pain in the ICU
where they scrape
operate
scrape
Her mother & relatives stand rigid vigil
as the doctors debate on whether to pull
her plug
He was mad about something
& every man can understand the lengths
to which a man can be driven by a woman
Maybe he thought she didn't
love him enough
or he was tired of her
or she hurt his feelings
or maybe she was just there
& he was in a bad mood
there was a can of gasoline around
& she wasn't paying close enough attention
to him
Ashamed we pray she dies because what life
could she make with feet, a small hank of hair
& pain
stretching unlimited until death

Poor & Indian to begin with
what disability check could provide a skin
of safety for her
He's in jail
he was out on bail for a murder
he could get out again
Filling up at the station
I almost vomit from the smell
She won't make the newspapers
like the central park jogger
Who cares about some Indian woman
with bad luck in boyfriends
I scrape my heart's dead tissue
Can't even weep anymore
having survived a thousand stories like
this one
Her hair blows across my eyes
She is walking barefoot on sweet clouds
I burn my arm accidentally shiver
with smaller pain that hisses her name
All's fair in love & war
Love & war are one
He was mad
at her
about something

Holiday

In overcast August after a big lunch outside
with 2 beautiful Butch friends laughing & teasing
We passed an overcoat bag lady
who is there all the time
I slipped her $3
'cause I had to buy gas
With the widest bright lights grin
she said *Merry Christmas!*
for the first time in my life
I liked those words

for Melanie Kaye/Kantrowitz

Back at the Ugly Motel

the supposed glamour crinkles with the cellophane
I strip from a plastic cup
throwing out the sound of clapping
which may or may not mean anything
but is definitely
another drug
to skirt
The silence is beige to match
the carpet, walls, drapes, couch with a slit in it
This has been the site of some wild
parties but tonight it's full of the dead air
of loneliness which has nothing to do
with being alone in the room
A bus & a taxi to catch in the morning
another plane the following day
This is probably why many
writers drink   Sounds of clinking ice
drown out the damage of microphones
questions from an audience who usually
don't understand
what we mean from our prison of language
lusting to be known, our tears made meaningful
our passion more than a 3-minute spray of juice
Crooked in sober misery I stare at the bland
white photo on the wall of empty jars crowded together
shouting *Art Art This is Art*
I turn restlessly remembering the janitor
sulking & waiting in the back of the hall
saying as I stood nearby
how sick he was of all this damn poetry

how brilliant his smile when he knew
we were all shut off
leaving in clots of fans & confusion
His relief & mine
shoved together in my dreams

for Bruce Jacobs

Soap Bubbles

When I was in high school, I wanted to be an actress.
I could cry on demand, which impressed my teacher.
I was pretty good at acting like someone else, but before
I could concentrate & become really fine, I noticed that
the only Indian on TV or in the movies was Jay
Silverheels, whose dialogue was not exactly inspiring. I
decided that, at least if I was a writer, I wouldn't have to
wait for anyone to call me before I could work. Today,
as a 47-year-old crank who will never get to be an
actress, I think about the nice Japanese couple on TV
who are advertising a bookcase system & realize that I
still don't see Indians on TV except to advertise trash
bags or to add ethnic color to white evening soaps
(which I watch just to see them). Of course, we didn't
even get that far until the last 10 years. I think about
Geronimo being played by Chuck Conners & about
Charlie Chan who was a white man. I know that no
Indian actress will be allowed to play Miss Marple,
which is no more absurd. There are no Indians alive on
daytime soaps, although for a while there was an "evil"
Asian woman, a schemer named Blair, who later came
back as a white woman. A miracle indeed, but soaps
are full of them. Black people are slightly more popular
than we are, though we'll never see a fine movie like
Daughters in the Dust on late night. I probably won't live
to see a time when schools won't have children painting
pictures of columbozo's boats "discovering" us. I'd be
really surprised if an Indian actress won an Oscar or
even played the lead in a movie where whites weren't
important at all. If Elizabeth Taylor & Claudette Colbert

can be Africans, why Meryl Streep could be Pocahontas.
Some people still wish we'd die off as quickly as
possible, as long as we leave behind all our good arts
& crafts. I've cried at hundreds of movies about white
people but I don't complain about it the way they do to
me when they read *Bury My Heart at Wounded Knee*.
Someplace in me, maybe in us, is closed over with grief
we have no words to speak. It's why we move so slowly.
This is not acting. Here we are. This is our land.
None of this makes any sense
does it?

for all Native actresses & actors

Stan Berg

in pain planted dozens & dozens of daffodils

using his own money

at the Country Club

where he worked

with only one hand

his other hurt in a fall

He lived to see them

one season

before he died of cancer

Correspondence with Troubled Souls Welcomed

Dear Grace & Truth Society my greatest trouble
is that I'm more concerned with truth
than the rent
My landlady wants her money
wants to raise the rent
I can barely raise the money
to pay the rent now
Dear Grace & Truth
Does jesus write checks payable
to bearer on demand
Does he pass out food stamps
extend credit   give unsecured loans
I have all the grace & truth I can stand
Truth being
whatever is
Grace being
the sun coming up every morning
Can't you give me some cold hard cash
calculated to relieve my troubled soul
in the here & now
I'm sure poets belong in heaven anyway
we're useless here on earth
I'm already *in* the hereafter
& if I don't eat soon
my body will join me
Dear Grace & Truth correspond my troubles away
If jesus can be cashed without an account
at this branch
I believe   I believe

in response to a pamphlet stuck in my door

Crazy Horse

I'm ironing a shirt with your name
blue 100% cotton the label says made in Macau
Your face melts under spray starch your eyes close
our connection frayed with Mohawk gas stations
Winnebago trucks, Navajo moving & storage
This is not my shirt, nor my kin's
While I iron it for her, she listens
to rock 'n roll & television at the same time
More than our hoop is broken
Surviving we drink their poison
to shut out their poisoning of our mother
I iron your name with bitter heat
my heart permanently pressed in anger
Our mother moans under the weight of cement
they want to choke her out of herself
Crazy Horse don't look
Our home shrunk to land stabbed with oil rigs
coal strippers, uranium mines
I could dampen this shirt with my tears
I could burn for hours before your name
still not cleanse this hatred
Crazy Horse I saw a book yesterday talking
about the brave
& daring conquest of the savage wild west
They're experts at calling murder any other name
Standing on the sidewalk I can't breathe
my feet scream for her soft embrace
Crazy Horse I'm glad you're dead
can't see the maggots nod with approval

Yesterday as we stood watching speakers
after the Gay Day Parade
a Black man threw a bottle of beer at us
screamed *What are you mother-fuckin' Indians*
doing here?!
Through clenched teeth I wondered
What is anybody doing here
but us
We're surviving
Names are sacred
they know that
Their copyright laws hungry with it
I want to iron Abraham Lincoln boxer shorts
I want to buy gas at a jesus christ station
I want to write with a Sojourner Truth pencil
Here is the iron
burnt arm of defeat
Here their smooth white cover
an invisible fire in the walls
Crazy Horse I want to sit beside you
be told how to live here
now that it's savage with greed
wild with locks
brave with destruction
Crazy Horse my iron heart is a broken blue hoop
burning in your steps

for Sandra Laronde

Honor Dance for the Four Winds

Because we are sacred to each other
you create a feast for us to share
placed carefully on newspaper
Each grain of rice
a memory of freedom
Each bean a song of respect
I am giving you all the stars I've seen
I am bringing you the moon in my voice
I am dancing you old mountains
Wind riding wild ponies
through canyons of our pain
I am covering each of you in a shawl
with long silky fringe & deeply colored roses
I am folding blankets for you
in blazing patterns
I carry you carefully in my eyes
on all my journeys
I dream nightly of the keys I will forge
of your loneliness, cradled smooth
Trapped in walls of hatred that I so rarely breach
listening for the birds who fly over razor wire coils
your spirits rise before me
I am burning sweet grass
sage & cedar
as each dawn I call your names

Back Road

is the way you came into my hills driving slowly
careful to promise nothing you could not give
Easy with my random wildness
No fence in your hands
Your body over mine is so sure
of each place which craves your mouth
Never gone so far with anyone riding
until I said stop
Held still by your voice
which drains my tears to laughter
As this evening
in the face of my broken mumbling
you told me of driving by a shorn corn field
after lunch break
to see flocks of white egrets
feasting in afternoon light
your amazement pure
as the way you take me
I turn in sleep
find they settle over me for the night
their feathers warm as your eyes
coming upon me
unsurprised

Stars

full generous in beauty hold me in tender light
Each one a burning kindness against the icy bite
All comfort comes from mystery we let be
shining without reason
across a thousand years of sky
simple as white primroses who open
all through winter
denying snow in shelter of a drooping fir
Each heart petal centered gold
as strangers exclaim my miracle
gift given as sweet sustenance
for grief more terror stained
than any want to bear
I planted these
rescued from bins of ignorance
They thrive as do I
in spite of chill cruel frosts echoed in her eyes
I've made my mother be
all that lives in rooted harmony
She whose blood carried me here
I've sent beyond the night
so I may laugh with stones & shells
hold shelter with my arms around a tree
whose old bark patterns my face with words
In my footsteps no child sings
my voice calls out alone
in darkness I name rest
This dandelion of my breath a silver promise
alive

Gathering Words

During my years of participation in First Nations battles
for sovereignty and justice, I've lived inside war. It is
a war that all Indians know but that very few others
respect or recognize. It is not a "simple" (I use this
term sarcastically) war of racism, which is the struggle
of other Peoples of Color living here, although we also
fight racism. This continent is morally and legally our
land, since no treaty has been observed. In order for a
government to claim a right to govern, it must have
clear title. In european history, wars have consistently
been waged for violation of treaties. Logically, then, we
remain at war in a unique way—not for a piece of the
"white pie," but because we do not agree that there is a
pie at all. The government works around the clock to
suppress the facts of this war (land theft, cultural &
spiritual appropriations, alcoholism, theft of children,
genocide) and its impact on us. War is *not* a metaphor.
Our fight is simply not broadcast on the 5 o'clock news
because an important part of our genocide is the myth
that we have all vanished into cupboards or are happy
somewhere selling crafts to tourists. We are not allowed
designated victim status because that would admit to the
worst instance of mass murder in world history. Our
invisibility is woven deeply into the shame of history.
We are continuously exploited in the media for images
of romance, savagery, stupidity and treachery. I seek to
pierce the white fog the mainstream media conjure
because I believe that when our truth is fully known,
we will have many allies in our war. These ideas are

not "mine;" they are the result of many discussions with other First Nations warriors.

We joke that there are far more FBIS (feds) than FBIS (full-blood Indians) & they're *still* scared to death. Every struggle we have waged for dignity or treaty rights has been violently attacked, often with traitors from the government who pose as "one of us," such as Douglas Durham. One of my jobs as a writer is to break their security.

Though I hate the word "victim," which implies helplessness, we are victims—unarmed sitting ducks— before we are born into the massive & deliberate campaign of lies which constitute the history of govern- ment & its controllers, the conglomerates which I call the greedy boys. I use this name to remind myself of their immature minds, which perceive life from a tiny hole called profits. I resist the use of the word "patriarchy" because (in true colonizer fashion) it obscures the nature of the truth. The greedy boys have only been on Turtle Island a little over 500 years. What we experience is not patriarchy, but the process of colonization, which immigrant women have profited from right along with the greedy boys. Patriarchy is only one of the many tools of colonizer mentality & is often used by women against other women.

I consciously fashion my writing as a weapon for my own survival & that of my allies. It has surprised me that my objective has often been overlooked by review- ers, who consistently reduce me to "feeling angry," when my purpose is so blatantly to shoot back in the old way, from the trees, in sneak attacks that masquerade as strings of artfully arranged words. This book's title, *Fire Power*, hopefully leaves no question as to my intent: I am a warrior against all forms of injustice. I intend to be one of the many hands insuring the survival of Indigenous People worldwide (by this I mean all colonized people, including Africans, whose situation has been cleverly masked so that they are not commonly referred to as Indigenous). These words are undeniably treason. I pledge nothing to a government that abuses us. A long time ago, a famous writer told me that my poem "I Walk in the History of My People" was not poetry because it was too political. I assert that poetry without politics is narcissistic & not useful to us. I also believe that everything is political—there is no neutral, safe place we can hide out in waiting for the brutality to go away.

Among the many joys of Indigenous Culture are puns & delight in multiple meanings. While English is one of the stiffer conqueror languages, I enjoy pushing it around. Thus, Fire Power is not only this book as a gun aimed at the "american canon," but is also about truth as fire and as power. It is seeing my life as a First Nations Two-Spirited Lesbian as fire & as power which can help heal our mother and ourselves. Poetry is the song of the people, not the painted bird of the academic machine. My most treasured response from listeners is, "I hate poetry, but I love yours!" This means that I have attained the sacred goal of writing & relationship— to communicate. My audiences are my allies in this war, a war in which all of us are victims, as all of us are colonized, although it is much harder to feel the war when we are far from the front & comfortably watching TV nonsense after a good meal.

This book holds many pieces of my personal struggle for survival from a violent, alcoholic family, & my subsequent imprisonments in psychiatric wards over a period of 10 years. My last incarceration was in January 1975. Writing this has helped me cauterize many old wounds & I hope it is useful to others who share this grief. I know well how common my experience has been. In sharing these dark shards, I hope to encourage others to bite open the bullet of pretense in which we live. Telling the truth is powerful medicine. It is a fire that lights the way for others. Truth has always been forbidden by governments, whose purpose is to exploit. When we speak our "Fire Power," we join a long & honored line of warriors against injustice.

Do not bother to feel guilty if your life may seem less difficult than mine. Use your ease to make the lives of others easier. As I have, as many women & men & children have, you can make your life a weapon against exploitation. It does not matter that we may not win our war to save our mother. It matters that we fight honorably for her. Those who rape her, who rape us, have no souls. In fighting them, we preserve our own. Poetry is a great force for healing, as Pat Parker first showed me many years ago. We are bombarded daily to ignore our true wounds. The mainstream media direct our focus on trivia, noise & tragedies about which we

can do nothing (which cleverly increases our feeling
of helplessness). My prayer is that these fragments of
my battle to become whole & sane (still ongoing)
will fire you to discover your power, which is often
misunderstood in western syphilization. Each of us is
born with innate power & purpose, a sacred direction
for which we have been created. Our task is to find
the place where we belong & do our work there. We
struggle against a vast conspiracy designed to rob us of
that power & redirect our energies into maintaining the
corporate consumer state for the profits of the rich.
Power is most dangerous when it is used against others;
like bullets, it has a habit of ricocheting. I recommend
that you give as much time as you can to being silently
reflective on our brainwashing, to writing or creating
your arsenal. I especially encourage other First Nations
women to record their stories in honor of the grief-
stricken silence of our ancestors who fought for our
lives. We live in a world which continuously erases us;
the process of bringing our thoughts into the material
world can be an important part of self-esteem. This is
how I've managed to stay alive. This cleans us of toxic
trivializations and allows our spirits room to sing. These
songs, like the songs of dawn birds, will begin our days
well. I wish you courage and the light of love to see
your way.

Chrystos was born off-reservation, in San Francisco, on November 7, 1946, of a Menominee father and a euro-immigrant mother. She is self-educated. She works for many political issues, among them: political prisoners in the u.s.a.; battering of heterosexual & lesbian women; land & treaty rights; anti-racism and queer safety. She is the winner of the following awards: National Endowment for the Arts Fellowship for Literature; Barbara Deming Memorial Grant; Lannan Foundation Grant for Poetry; Audre Lorde International Poetry Competition; and the Fund for Human Rights Freedom of Expression Award (with Minnie Bruce Pratt & Audre Lorde). In 1995, she received the Sappho Award of Distinction from the Astraea National Lesbian Action Foundation.

Her writing is widely anthologized, and *Fire Power* is her fifth book. She still travels too much giving readings, lectures, keynote speeches & writing workshops. Her home on Bainbridge Island is a tiny cabin overlooking the Puget Sound, where her large gardens keep her out of trouble & chronically late for deadlines. She is grateful to Creation for the gift of life, for the ability to write & draw, & for her relationships.

Press Gang Publishers has been producing vital and
provocative books by women since 1975.

A free catalogue of our books in print is available from
Press Gang Publishers, 101-225 East 17th Avenue,
Vancouver, B.C. V5V 1A6 Canada